WHAT PEOPLE AR

Above ↗

• • • •

"*Above All Else* is a perfect follow-up to *Twelve Pillars*. How often do we get to jump forward and see how someone succeeded thirty years after getting advice that will change their life? In Chris' new book, it is exciting to see how the lessons learned, and new lessons as well, can change a life and leave a legacy for others. Enjoy this simple story of success."

—Jim Rohn, America's Foremost
Business Philosopher

• • • •

"Success is not achieved by what you pursue, but rather who you become. This poignant story not only tells you what to do; more important, it shows you how to be."

—Darren Hardy, Publisher of *SUCCESS* magazine,
www.SUCCESS.com

. . . .

"Chris Widener has written another little gem with a message that is needed now more than ever. With so many challenged and trying not to lose hope, matters of the heart are essential to survive and thrive. This book will give you the insights you need to keep your heart healthy and your confidence strong."

—Mark Sanborn, best-selling author of
The Fred Factor, The Encore Effect
and *You Don't Need a Title to Be a Leader*

. . . .

"In *Above All Else*, we are reminded of the most important aspect of success and life—keeping our heart in the right place. Follow the lessons of this little book, and you will not only achieve success, you will enjoy it!"

—Jeffrey Fox, author of *Rain: What a Paperboy Learned About Business*

. . . .

"Chris continues his classic series with *Above All Else*, tapping into the wisdom of Solomon for a deeper connection with the heart. Michael moves from learning the Twelve Pillars to paying it forward for his grandson. This message really spoke to me about where I am in my journey!"

—Donna Johnson, www.SpiritWings.com

. . . .

"It's amazing the impact that Chris' book *Twelve Pillars* has had, and continues to have, on our team. Chris' books are timeless. Every time you read or reread one of them, you're sure to find something new. It's very rare that a sequel is better than the original, but I believe Chris has done it!"

—Ryan D. Chamberlin,
Team National—Double Platinum
Presidential Director

. . . .

"Once again, Chris Widener inspires us to soul-search into the wisdom of the ages in order to connect the dots of our own destiny and to empower others to do the same."

—David Humphrey, President, ILD Global

. . . .

"I have known fabulous wealth and tremendous success, and I have had my share of failure as well. Through it all, I learned firsthand the lessons of *Above All Else*: The most important thing in life is the state of your heart. I highly recommend Chris Widener's new book!"

—Bill Bartmann, author of *Bailout Riches*,
www.BillBartmann.com

. . . .

"Just when I thought Chris couldn't top his previous books, he delivers a home run. *Above All Else* is a fun, quick, and practical guide to success based on the most ancient and time-tested principles. I love the story format that Chris uses to teach such incredible lessons! Read it, learn from it, and then share it!"

—Ron White, memory expert, National Memory Champion, www.MemoryInAMonth.com

. . . .

"There is a reason that passed-along wisdom is so valuable—because it stands the test of time! This book is worth more gold than has ever been mined."

—Greg S. Reid, author of *Three Feet from Gold*

. . . .

"In *Above All Else*, you will learn how to leave a legacy of great significance and success. You'll discover in this delightful story how to live with your heart and make a difference at the same time!"

—Jim Cathcart, www.Cathcart.com, author of *The Acorn Principle*

. . . .

"*Above All Else* may well be one of the, if not
the most, important little books you will ever
read! This book will move you, challenge
you, and delight you, all in a short 90-minute
read! Caution: Permanent success and endless
happiness will occur as a result of reading this
book. Read only if these are dear to your heart!"
— Donna Krech, The Donna Krech Companies,
www.DonnaKrech.com

. . . .

"There is little that can be said about brilliance.
It speaks for itself. This book is brilliant. Chris
and I met several years ago, and I was blown
away not only by his gifts, but also by his
humility. This book is a must-read for anyone
who desires more in life, but also more out of
life. Above all else, read this book. It will elevate
you beyond all expectations to heights that most
only dream of. Bravo, Chris!"
— Doug Firebaugh, author, speaker, trainer,
www.DougFirebaugh.com

"If you yearn for pure happiness and success in your life, then this book is for you. Chris has done a stellar job writing a captivating story that will touch your heart and soul. This book will change your life."
—Manny Goldman, author of *The Power of Personal Growth,* www.PersonalGrowth.com

"This book 'wowed' me, and I could not put it down! It's a great story that teaches a powerful lesson, which gives you the key to creating lifelong success! Read and reread this book. Then, get a copy for every friend and family member! It's a gift that will change their lives!"
—James Malinchak, co-author of *Chicken Soup for the College Soul,* www.BigMoneySpeaker.com

"*Above All Else* is a great little read that brings to life a very important truth: Success in life is not at all about material wealth or power; it is about your heart and how you live out your priorities."
—Lonnie Pacelli, author of *Why Don't They Follow Me? 12 Easy Lessons to Boost Your Leadership Skills,* www.Follow-Me-Book.com

· · · ·

"This book's message could not be more
relevant, timely, and important for society today.
People in every home, office, or school can find a
nugget that will change their heart forever."

—Dianna Booher, CEO, Booher Consultants,
www.Booher.com

· · · ·

"*Above All Else* gets to the center of living a
good life: what's in your heart. Chris Widener's
book will touch your heart and teach you how
to protect your most valuable treasure—the
inner you."

—Joe Calloway, author of *Becoming a
Category of One*, www.JoeCalloway.com

· · · ·

"Chris shares principles that can serve as a
road map in uncertain times. His message on
achieving success includes the capacity each
of us has to create more meaning, joy, and
fulfillment in our lives—at any time we choose.
It couldn't come at a better time!"

—Michael Walsh, President, High Performers
International, Inc.

"*Above All Else* is a wonderfully inspiring and insightful book that reminds us all about what truly matters in life. This book will touch your heart and empower you on your path of success and fulfillment."

—Mike Robbins, CSP, author of *Be Yourself: Everyone Else Is Already Taken*, www.Mike-Robbins.com

. . . .

"Above all else, read this book, because it gets to the heart of the matter, no matter what's the matter, and that's what matters most. Knowledge is not power. Wisdom is. And the wisdom in *Above All Else* is very powerful!"

—John Milton Fogg, author of *The Greatest Networker in the World*

. . . .

"Chris Widener is a masterful storyteller who has a unique way of impacting your head while touching your heart. *Above All Else* made me reflect on my life on a very deep level and inspired me to rethink how I define success. This book is a gem."

—Waldo Waldman, www.YourWingman.com

. . . .

"Chris Widener's newest work is an entertaining, yet poignant, tale about the importance of focusing your heart on what really matters. Your focus dictates your direction, so if you concentrate on yourself first, success has a solid foundation on which to take root and grow."
—Laura Stack, productivity expert, author, and professional speaker, www.TheProductivityPro.com

. . . .

"Chris Widener has written what is sure to become a success classic. The easy-to-read style in which it is written pulls you in, but the powerful, life-changing lessons it imparts will stay fresh in your mind long past the time it takes you to read this wonderful book. The ideas shared have the ability to change your life, both personally and professionally. Read it, study it, put the ideas in it into practice in your life, and you will be infinitely better for having done so."
—Josh Hinds, speaker, author, entrepreneur; Founder, www.GetMotivation.com

. . . .

"How true, to achieve lasting success, you must take care of your heart. Chris brilliantly entertains us, but most important, he helps us to take a look at how we should, 'above all else,' guard our heart!"

—April Humphrey, Executive VP, ILD Global,
www.ILDGlobal.com

. . . .

"What a surprise read! This isn't just a great story; it's a book of wise counsel that I'm having my 11-year-old son read. He can have a head start on personal and professional success that I worked for over decades."

—Dan Seidman,
One of America's Top Sales Coaches

· · · ·

"Another great read from one of the best in the business. In the spirit of Og Mandino, *Above All Else* takes you on a trip that doesn't disappoint. The story reveals crisp, clear, concise lessons that everyone can use (and most need to be reminded of occasionally), shared in a way that makes you put yourself in the story—walking along the beach with your grandfather and learning the lessons he learned in his lifetime. You'll want to pass this one along to those you care about and who are looking for their pathway to success. And spend some time discussing it with them. It's a winner!"

—Michael Hudson, Ph.D.,
www.MichaelHudson.com

· · · ·

"*Above All Else* draws you in and sends a powerful message straight to your heart. It's one of those books that you just can't wait to share with your friends and family—a captivating story, timeless principles, and the 'oomph' to nudge you in the right direction for achieving and enjoying true success."

—Rich Fettke, author of Extreme Success,
www.Fettke.com

CHRIS WIDENER

Author of the best-selling book
Twelve Pillars with Jim Rohn

ABOVE ALL ELSE

The Single **Most Important Lesson** for
Achieving, Sustaining, and Enjoying Success

SB

To my wife, Lisa,
who guards her heart better than anyone I know.

SB

INTRODUCTION

· · · ·

Throughout history, countless books have shared important ideas about success. Many claimed to have the secret or key to success—and many embody great ideas. But throughout my quest for the same important ideas about success, I kept coming back to a piece of ancient wisdom, a proverb from the Old Testament written by the richest man of all time, Solomon. His name is synonymous with wealth and wisdom. It begins, "Above all else...."

We can scour all of the world's literature and try to find the secret to success; we can devour the biographies of billionaires; we can stand in awe of the stories of Olympic athletes; we can be amazed at the lessons from those who have overcome incredible obstacles. But when the most successful man in human history starts out a sentence with "Above all else...," it is time for us to stop, listen, and reflect on his advice.

So, what should we do, "above all else?" I seek to answer that question in this book. It has been a challenge to learn and implement Solomon's wisdom into my own life. In my research, I received insights from some of the most successful men and women I've met on how they apply this principle in their own lives. Their thoughts are included in this story.

The characters and story are based on characters Jim Rohn and I created for our best-selling book *Twelve Pillars*. You will get an overview of *Twelve Pillars*, principles Jim and I think should be a part of everyone's life early on in this book as a refresher, or in case you haven't read it.

You'll notice that the subtitle for this novel is very deliberate. It says this book is "the single most important lesson for achieving, sustaining, and enjoying success." I've found that most books focus on achieving success.

The principle you will learn here will go even further: It will make sure that you enjoy your success once you get there. Just open the newspaper, and you will see people who have achieved fame and fortune, yet do not enjoy it. I believe they learned how to achieve success but failed to learn to enjoy or sustain it. That is the key: Get it. Keep it. Enjoy it.

Thanks for picking up *Above All Else*. I hope you will benefit from reading it as much as I did in writing it.

— Chris Widener

CHAPTER

I

· · · ·

Michael Jones was walking down the beach on his beloved Sanibel Island. He and his wife Amy had lived an incredible life, and now, at age seventy-two, he was enjoying the fruit of that life. A number of years ago they had built their dream home on West Gulf Drive on this exquisite tropical island. It was a sprawling estate built on three lots, with a cost of over ten million dollars. It had a gorgeous view to the south, looking out to the seemingly endless horizon. Dolphins regularly swam just off the beach. Birds were plenty. And most of all, Michael loved the shells—a nearly endless beach of incredible shells. He loved to walk and look for another perfect shell for his collection. He and Amy enjoyed the hand-in-hand walks they took together, but this evening, Michael was by himself. It was just before sunset, and he was walking toward the setting sun. His heart was filled with the wonder of it all.

His peace was temporarily broken when his cell phone rang. He normally didn't bring it with him on his walks, but he forgot to take it out of his back pocket before he left. When he saw who it was on his caller I.D., he was glad he had it. It was his oldest grandchild, Josh.

He punched the connect button. "Josh! How are you?"

"Good, Grandpa. How are you?"

"I am doing terrific. Just walking along the beach, enjoying the sunset. What are you up to?"

"Just doing homework." It was September of Josh's senior year of high school, and he was inundated by the workload. Josh was a good kid—a strong young man with a good head on his shoulders and a bright future. Since Michael and Amy had moved full time to Sanibel Island, Josh hadn't seen as much of his grandparents. Usually just a week a year for vacations. But Josh and Michael spoke on the phone every couple of weeks.

"What classes are you taking? You are a senior this year, right?"

"Yep. One year to go. I am taking the normal stuff. Pre-Calculus, English, History. You know."

"Well, your grandpa is getting up there. It was over fifty years ago when I was in high school. Are you enjoying it?"

"Actually I am. I am just trying to make sure I do well in school and also have some fun with my friends. You know what they say, 'All work and no play makes Johnny a dull boy.'"

"Just like your grandpa, Josh."

"Well, Grandpa, I am calling because of one class I am taking. It requires me to do a senior project on a successful person."

"Yeah, who are you going to do it on?"

"Well, I was thinking about doing it on you, Grandpa."

"Well, that's very flattering, Josh, but you should do it on a president or one of the great industrialists or technology titans. That's probably what your teacher expects. A historical figure."

"Well, I asked my teacher if I could do it on you, and she said yes. I mean, Grandpa, lots of people know you, and you have achieved more than almost everybody. And the fact is, even though I know your basic rags-to-riches story, I don't even know the details behind it. I've picked up bits and pieces throughout the years, but maybe now would be the time for me to put it all together."

Indeed, Michael had achieved more than most Americans, but it hadn't always been that way. At forty years old he was broke, but at age sixty-four, he sold his company for a three billion dollar profit and walked away into retirement. For twenty years, he had been a regular fixture on the cover of business magazines, so many people knew his name and his basic story.

Michael was proud that his grandson would want to know about his life. "If your teacher says it is okay, then, okay. What do I need to do to help you?"

"Awesome. Well, I just need to interview you. I need to tell your life story, but this is really more about what drives you. All the kids have to write about a successful person but not just what they did. We have to write, as my teacher calls it, 'the story behind the story.' Would that be okay?"

"It sounds great to me. Hey, I have an idea. How about I fly you down here one weekend next month, and you and I can spend the weekend together? We can fish and go out on the boat and do your project."

"That would be great. I have to ask my dad, though."

"You leave your dad to me. We'll have you come down on a Thursday night and go home Sunday night."

"But what about school on Friday?"

"Josh, there is an old saying: 'Don't let school get in the way of your education.' What you will learn that Friday will be more important than your entire high-school curriculum, combined."

"Okay, if you can get my mom and dad to let me. That would be fun."

"We'll get it done. This will be fun! You tell me the dates you want to come, and I'll buy the ticket."

"Wow. That'll be great, Grandpa."

"It sure will, Josh."

"I'll let you know."

"All right. Love ya, buddy."

"You too, Grandpa. Bye."

When they hung up, Michael slid his phone back into his pocket. He kept walking, his heart warmer than the evening sun. When he got back to the house, he shared the news with Amy. She was ecstatic to be able to have one of her grandchildren come down. She was also happy that Michael would be able to tell his story one-on-one with one of his grandchildren. Though Michael had become a famous person, he was also a private person. Somewhat of an introvert. Just as Josh had said, Michael's children and grandchildren knew the basic story of what had happened, but Michael had never really gone into great detail about the intricacies of his life and transformation from broke salesman to billionaire.

Michael and Amy waited eagerly at the passenger reception area at the Southwest Florida International Airport three weeks later. It had been about four months since they had seen Josh, and they were excited to have him down for the weekend. As promised, Michael had talked Josh's dad into letting him out of school to spend the weekend in Florida. And just to make sure he was covered, Josh talked with his teachers. They were all on board with his absence to further his senior project.

When Josh came out through the roped-off area, he had a big smile on his face. "Hey, Grandma and Grandpa!" They rushed together and hugged, Amy first.

"Did you check your bag or carry it on?" Michael asked.

"I just brought this one big backpack," Josh replied. "So we are good to go."

"Great. We are so excited to have you here this weekend," Amy exclaimed.

They walked out to Michael and Amy's SUV and settled in for the forty-five minute drive to their home. They got all caught up on everything that was going on in their lives. Josh updated them on his brothers and sisters and everything they were involved in. By the time they arrived at home, it was past ten o'clock. Michael scooped some ice cream for the three of them and snuggled in on the couch as he told Josh what would be happening in the next few days.

About ten-thirty, he called it a night. "So, you are up in the first guest room on the left upstairs. Make yourself at home. We will leave about eight for some fishing. It's about ten minutes down to the marina. Then we can get started on your school project. I have been racking my brain to make sure I give you all the good stuff."

"Sounds good, Grandpa. I'll see you in the morning," he said as he bounded up the stairs.

"I'll have breakfast ready at seven forty-five. Pancakes!" Amy called to Josh as he disappeared.

Michael and Amy sat together in the living room a few more minutes.

"I am so proud of you, Michael."

"Oh yeah? Why?"

"Just all that you have accomplished and the family we have. We have great kids and grandchildren."

"That we do."

"And I'm glad that you are going to spend some time with Josh telling him all of the things that you have learned over the years. I know how important they have been to you. Now is a good time to make sure your family knows them."

"Yes, I've tried over the years to talk to the kids, but I never wanted to be pushy. They need to learn for themselves."

"Well, you have earned the right to be heard. You will have a good time, and Josh will learn a lot. And it will strengthen the bond between you."

"I hope so." Michael stood up. "You ready to go to bed, young lady?"

Amy smiled. She knew she was no longer a "young lady," but that is what Michael insisted on calling her. "I sure am, sweetheart." They walked slowly down the hall to go to bed.

Seven-thirty came soon enough, and the clock radio woke Josh from a sound sleep. His grandma and grandpa had the best beds, even in their guest rooms. That's one of the perks of being wealthy. He took a quick shower, threw on his boating clothes and some sunscreen and headed downstairs for his grandma's famous pancakes, along with bacon and fruit. On most school days, he got a bowl of cereal. He devoured this feast.

By eight-fifteen, Michael and Josh were boarding Michael's yacht, Second Chance. It was a gorgeous seventy-seven-foot Hatteras Convertible Sportfishing Yacht. Josh had never seen it before, so this was new to him.

"Let's take her down off of Naples and Marco for some fishing, Skip." The captain's name was Bob, but Michael always called him "Skip," short for Skipper.

"Will do, boss," Skip replied.

Once out in the waters off of Naples, they pulled the rods and reels out of the storage bin, got them ready and in the water. "Okay, you fish. Jump on the lines," Michael shouted. The waters off of the coast were filled with grouper, Spanish mackerel, tuna, and many other kinds of fish.

They waited for the action to begin.

As they sat in the sun, the temperature hovering around seventy-eight degrees, enjoying the view of the water, and drinking iced tea, Josh decided to get down to business. He pulled out a little digital recorder and set it on the table between him and his grandpa. "Mind if I record you while I ask some questions?"

"No, not at all. But don't you want to just write this stuff down? Or will you do it later?"

"Write it down? Grandpa, the pencil went out with your generation. I'll dump the audio file for this into my computer, run it through voice recognition software, and it will write it for me." Josh had a big smile on his face. Michael was astounded.

"They can do that now?" he asked. "I always heard it was coming but didn't know it was here."

"Grandpa, you owned the largest consumer electronics chain in the world. You sold this stuff!"

"Josh, I have been out of the game a few years. We didn't sell this kind of technology. It was on the horizon, but it's a brand-new world for you and your generation." How the world was changing.

Josh pushed the record button and began.

"So, Grandpa, how did you get so successful? What's the 'story behind the story'?"

Michael closed his eyes and tilted his head upward. Now was time for a trip down memory lane. "You know, I didn't start out as a success, either financially or otherwise. My life was pretty much a bust by the time I was forty."

"I knew that, but what changed?"

"Fortunately, my car broke down." He looked at his grandson. He knew that would stump him. "More accurately, I thought it had broken down."

"Your life changed and you became a success because you thought your car broke down?"

Michael laughed. "Yeah, that's the way it happened." He looked away from Josh and out over the water. He wondered how his life would have turned out if he hadn't run out of gas that day. "You see, there is the old saying: 'When the student is ready, the teacher will appear.' I guess I was ready."

"What happened?"

"I was about forty. Your grandma and I were struggling to get by. I was barely making any money. Your dad was about eleven and your Aunt Jennifer was nine or so. I was driving to a sales call, driving along a road in the middle of nowhere, when my car broke down. Ran out of gas, actually. But I thought at the time it had broken down. Only thing that broke was the gas gauge, though. I walked up to this house I had stopped in front of. It was a huge mansion, actually. I had never seen anything like it in person. It sat behind a huge gate. The name of the house was Twelve Pillars."

"The house had a name?"

"Yep. Twelve Pillars. I'll get to why in a little bit. So, anyway, I was looking through this gate, and I saw the maintenance man. An old guy named Charlie. He got me back on the road again. Helped me figure out I just needed some gas. And, he changed my life."

"I have heard the term Twelve Pillars before. Dad or you must have mentioned it. But let's talk about this: A maintenance man at a mansion in the middle of nowhere changed your life?" This was fast becoming an interesting story.

Just then a fish hit the line, pulling the tip way down. "Got one on your rod, Josh. Pull him in." Josh jumped up and started playing the fish. A few minutes later, he pulled in a huge red grouper. Michael was overjoyed. "That is going to make for some good eating!"

They threw the fish in the hold tank, got the rod baited again, and sat back down to talk.

"Where were we?" Michael asked. "Oh, yes. The maintenance man. Yes sir, Josh, a maintenance man changed my life forever. Want to know how?"

"That's why I'm here."

"He taught me the Twelve Pillars of Success that the man who lived in the mansion, Mr. Davis, lived by. Took him a few months and a few more visits, but eventually he taught them to me and I took them for myself, began to apply them. And they changed my life."

"What were they? Life lesson stuff?"

"You could say that. There were twelve, but a couple really stood out for me."

"What are those?"

"You are lucky I memorized them. And you should, too. Here they are:

1. "Work Harder on Yourself Than You Do on Your Job

2. Live a Life of Health

3. The Gift of Relationships

4. Achieve Your Goals

5. The Proper Use of Time

6. Surround Yourself with the Best People

7. Be a Lifelong Learner

8. All of Life Is Sales

9. Income Seldom Exceeds Personal Development

10. Communication Brings the Common Ground of Understanding

11. The World Can Always Use One More Great Leader

12. Leave a Legacy"

"Wow, sounds like it covers almost everything. Did any of them mean more to you than the others?"

"Actually, there were two specifically that I really remember hitting me right between the eyes. One, work harder on yourself than you do on your job, and two, your income rarely exceeds your personal development. What Charlie the maintenance man taught me was that if I wanted my life to change, I had to change. Best advice I ever got. I stopped playing the victim of circumstances, took responsibility for my life, and turned my life around. I took some risks, started my own business, and it took off from there."

"Well, I would like to focus in on those Twelve Pillars, maybe. That would make a big part of the story, wouldn't it?"

"You should certainly include them, and maybe even write some on each one, but the big part of your story should be what I learned after I learned the Twelve Pillars."

"After the Twelve Pillars? Like what, the Thirteenth Pillar?"

"Well, I have never called it that, but there was one lesson I learned after Charlie passed away that really put all the pieces together. In fact, I would say it is the single most important lesson for achieving, sustaining, and enjoying my success. That is what I want to spend my time on with you. For two reasons: One, it will be a good story for your senior project, and two, you need to learn this yourself, Josh."

"Why do I need to learn it?"

"Because I love you and it is the most important thing you can do for yourself. I couldn't imagine one of my loved ones not knowing this. I am actually sorry I haven't been better at communicating this to your dad and aunt and you kids before." He paused and looked away from the boat, a touch of regret that he hadn't been more proactive about this before. He turned and looked back at Josh, his eyes visibly wet. "But now is the time I can share what I have learned with you."

Again the reels spun. Both at the same time. They both had fish on. For the next forty-five minutes, they barely got their lines in the water after pulling out the previous fish than they were reeling in more. They were going to eat well that night. At the end of the flurry of fish, they decided to eat lunch. Amy had prepared a lunch for them and they moved into the salon just off the stern of the boat. Michael retrieved the meal from the galley refrigerator and laid it out on the table for them to eat. Roast beef sandwiches, chips, apples, and soda for both of them. Homemade cookies for dessert.

After he took his first bite, Josh started again, his recorder in between the two. "So, Grandpa, what's this big lesson?"

"The most important lesson, Josh."

"Okay, the most important lesson. Let's hear it."

"Well, it is ancient wisdom. It comes from the richest man to ever live. His name was Solomon. He makes me look like a pauper. Very wealthy. But more important than that is that he is also considered the wisest man who ever lived. As the story goes, God gave him the choice of wealth or wisdom and he chose wisdom. Because of that choice, God gave him both. So, when I read what he said was the most important aspect of success, I decided I would live my life based on that principle."

"So what is it?" Josh asked, leaning forward.

"Here is what he said: 'Above all else, guard your heart, for it is the wellspring of life.'"

"That's it? I don't get it. Guard your heart? That's the greatest secret of your success?"

"That is indeed it, Josh. And, frankly, I didn't get it myself for a long time. For the first forty years of my life, I had no idea how to live life successfully. Then I met Charlie and he taught me the Twelve Pillars of Success. That would be a turning point for me. It got me started on the road of personal development and was the impetus for me to get started in my own business. But there were still challenges ahead."

"Like what challenges?"

"Well, I began to get very successful in business. I had learned what to do and I began doing it passionately. It paid off. I started making $100,000 a year. Then it was $250,000. Then a million dollars. Then, when we started opening up so many stores, it was money beyond my wildest imagination."

"Cool! So what's wrong with that?"

Michael laughed. "Yes, I know that kind of money sounds great to you. But there were other problems. Not money problems. Something far greater. I had heart problems."

"Really? I didn't know that. So you went to the doctor? Do you still take medicine?"

Michael smiled again. "No, not those kinds of heart problems. Not my physical heart. I have actually been fortunate that way. No health problems for the most part. I had different kinds of heart problems. Have you ever given much thought to your heart Josh?"

"You mean, like my soul?

"Yes, that is another word for it, I suppose. Philosophers and theologians have talked and written for millennia about what the heart is. There is the physical heart, of course, but they have also talked about that inner part of us that controls who we are. An analogy that helped me make sense of it is the difference between the brain and the mind. The brain is the physical part, but the mind is the nonphysical part that exists and drives us. It is similar with the heart. You have the physical heart, which sits at the core or center of your body, but then you have your heart, which, though not physical, is at the core of who we are and what we do. Does that make sense?"

"Yeah, that makes sense. The physical and the nonphysical." Josh thought for a moment. "So, what do you think the heart is anyway? Is it the soul? Is it the mind?"

"Okay, this is where I am limited, and really I don't think one has to get too deep on this. I am a businessman, not a philosopher. And really, for most of us, we only need a basic understanding of the heart in order to apply the really important lessons. I guess, for my application of it, I just considered it all wrapped up into one. The mind, the will, the emotions, the soul, the heart. It may not be technically right, but for lack of a better word, it is the 'me' that isn't physical. It is my morals and values, my ethics. It is my courage, my fear; it is the spiritual part of me. It is that intangible, internal force that drives me."

"I can go with that. So how does this 'wisdom,' as you call it, make a difference in your life?"

"Good question. You have to understand where I was personally at the time. I had figured the money part out, but I hadn't figured the heart part of life out. We moved into a beautiful home, bought new cars, traveled on fancy vacations, but I was, for lack of a better word, empty."

"Empty?"

"Yes. I had achieved success, but I didn't enjoy it. I didn't have money problems, but I had heart problems. I realized that I had the outside part looking good—at least in others' eyes—but I had issues with my heart. I knew that for me to sustain and enjoy my success, for me to achieve what I really wanted to achieve in life, I needed to address the issues of my heart."

They had both finished their food, and Skip came in to see if Michael wanted to stay where they were or move somewhere else.

"Let's move south of Marco Island and see what we can catch down there."

"Will do." Skip turned on his heels to head back to the wheel.

"Well, Josh, let's get back out there and get prepared to get those lines back in the water. We can talk more, or maybe we'll just fish and talk about this later."

"Sounds good. Either way, Grandpa."

Michael decided to just fish the rest of the afternoon. He enjoyed the time with Josh. He was very happy with how his grandchildren were turning out. They were definitely much further along than he was at their age.

They caught seven "keeper" fish that day, more than enough for a few good meals. By late afternoon, they were back at the marina and headed home. Michael felt good about the day, and Josh felt like he was starting to get what drove his grandpa.

CHAPTER
III

After a dinner of fresh fish with Amy, Michael and Josh went out for a walk on the beach. They turned right onto the beach, walking in the direction of Captiva Island. The beach in front of Michael's home was mostly sand, but there was a large strip of shells as you got closer to the water. Josh had forgotten his sandals, so they walked on the sand.

"Let's talk some more about this issue of the heart," Michael suggested.

"Okay, because I have been thinking about it. I get—sort of—what the heart is, but the thing you said about the rich guy.... 'Guard the well,' or something like that.... What does that mean?"

"Close, but no cigar. Here is what he said, and it's important to get it right. 'Above all else, guard your heart, for it is the wellspring of life.' "

"That's it. What's it mean?"

"Well, let's think about it. I actually think it says a lot. Josh, what is your number one priority in life?"

"Right now? Just getting through high school and getting into college."

"Is that it? What else is a priority for you?"

"Making some money to pay for gas and fun stuff I want to do."

"Anything else?"

"Hanging out with my friends."

"Is that it?"

"Probably not fighting with my brothers and sisters," he said with a smile. Michael thought that was funny, too.

"I hear you on that. So, those are your priorities? That's what you focus on?"

"Yeah, that's about it. Let me guess, that's not what I should be focusing on?"

"Oh, those things are fine. Good even. I am glad you are focusing on those things. But here is what I learned. The words 'above all else.' When I read those words for the first time, I came to a crisis of priorities. I realized that there can be only one thing that is above all else. There can be only one thing that takes precedence over all others. I had to ask, 'What is the single most important thing I could be doing?' and 'What is my ultimate priority?' The answer and the rationale for it are found in the rest of that little proverb. The what: Guard your heart. The why: Because your heart is the wellspring of life."

Josh looked down at the recorder in the pocket of his t-shirt. He hoped it was picking all this up. He looked back at his grandfather. "So explain how that changed you so much. What did that mean for you?"

Michael saw a potential shell, bent down to pick it up, realized it was too chipped to keep, and threw it back into the Gulf of Mexico before answering. "Let me start with the second first. I had never thought about my heart being the 'wellspring' of my life. I had never really thought about the fact that what was going on in my heart had a direct effect on both whether I achieved success and whether or not I would be able to sustain it and enjoy it. I was achieving it, but in hindsight, I really don't think I could have sustained it, mainly because I wasn't enjoying it.

"I had to take a deep look into my own heart, my soul if you will, and assess what was going on there. Your grandmother and I weren't getting along very well, I was frustrated, money didn't seem to bring me peace, and I was still distant from my kids...." Michael drifted off into silence, remembering where he had been so many years ago. Josh said nothing, not knowing what to say.

Michael began again. "What I realized was that my heart was stale. It had grown cold and hard. There was no life in it. It had been robbed of the joy and wonder that had been in it as a child. To further the metaphor, it was an empty well. There was no water to draw from, so to speak, to provide life for me. There was a well there, but it was dry. I realized that everyone has a well, but we determine whether it is dry or full."

Josh knew that his grandfather was saying something profound, but as a relatively young man, he didn't quite get it yet. Part of the wisdom comes from the experience of life. And that, Josh was short on.

"So you talked about the second part first. Now how about the first part second?" Josh asked.

"Right. Once I realized that the heart is the wellspring of life and that mine was empty, it made even more sense to me, the first part. Guard your heart. That is an interesting order. Guard it. Like something was trying to steal it. And then it hit me: All sorts of things try to steal our heart. They are the foes of the heart."

"Foes?"

"Yes. The things that are at war against the proper care and feeding of the heart. Foes. Enemies. There are lots of them."

"Really?"

"Yes, really. You are still young, Josh. Nothing wrong with that. In fact, sometimes I see how vibrant and strong and healthy you are, and I wish I was seventeen again. I realized that there are foes to the heart and that the best way to make sure those foes didn't overtake my heart and cause it to stray was for me to focus."

"An alliteration," Josh noted.

"A what?" his grandfather replied, having not heard him well.

"An alliteration. I learned it in my vocabulary studies. Alliteration: The repetition of the first consonant sound in a phrase. Focus and foes. Makes it easy to remember."

"I had never thought of that before. You're pretty smart."

"The apple doesn't fall far from the tree," Josh suggested.

"So let's go with that," Michael continued. Focus and foes." He turned and looked at Josh. "I'll have to find more words that begin with that to explain the other things I want to tell you. So, let me talk to you a little about the focus before I talk to you about the foes. I came to realize that my heart was focused on the wrong thing. It was focused on material success. I had gotten so tired of being broke that my whole goal was to get rich. And when the money started to come, I got even more focused on wealth. One night I was watching television—some entertainment news show or something

I saw flipping through the channels—and there was a story about some young movie star whose life was falling apart. Of course, that story is repeated so often as to be almost cliché. The thought struck me: This person's success was bigger than their heart and it needed to be the other way around.

"But what struck me even deeper was that I was the same way. My success was getting bigger than my heart. The heart has to be the foundation for our success in order for it to be sustainable and enjoyable. If the foundation isn't strong, eventually the whole house comes tumbling down, which is what you see almost every night on the news. Some movie star, politician, businessperson, minister—it can happen to anyone—their success falls apart because they didn't tend to the cultivation of their heart. Their focus was on their success, and their success grew. Then it weighs too much for the heart to contain it and it bursts. The whole thing implodes. Jesus asked what it profited a person to gain the entire world, yet lose their soul.

"I realized I was on that track. My success was growing, almost exponentially, but my heart was withering away. I was busy. I was enamored with my new wealth. But it wasn't good. So I decided I needed to focus on the growth of my heart as a foundation for my future success."

"So what did you do?"

"I started looking at disciplines that I put into my life that would allow my heart to grow."

"In other words, you looked for ways to foster it."

"Yes, you could say that. That works."

"And it starts with an 'F.'"

"Hey, you're getting pretty good with that. In order to overcome the foes of our hearts, we have to focus on its development and foster its growth. Pretty good, huh?"

"Yep. We make a good team."

"We may be getting ahead of ourselves, though. I have one more thought on focus."

"Oh, okay." At this point they had walked a half mile or so down the beach and decided to turn back.

Michael continued. "One Sunday, I was sitting in church and the minister quoted something Jesus said about the heart. It was the perfect thing to go with the proverb about guarding your heart. And it is all about focus."

"What did it say?" Josh asked.

"You know, let's wait until we get back and I can show it to you. Deal?"

"Sure, sounds good." They spent the rest of the walk back looking at the beautiful homes along West Gulf Drive and talking about one of their other favorite subjects, hockey. Josh had played hockey his whole life and was looking forward to his senior year playing for his high-school hockey team.

CHAPTER

IV

. . . .

A my welcomed them home as they came through the door. "Did you boys have a nice walk? It was a beautiful night for one."

"It sure was," Michael said. Didn't find any shells, though. Morning is best."

"We had a good talk. I am learning lots about Grandpa."

"Well, that's good. He has a lot inside of him." She came up beside Michael and gave him a hug. That's my man, your grandpa." Michael and Amy smiled at each other. "Hey, who wants some hot cocoa?"

Josh and Michael both said "me" at the same time. Amy went off to make some.

Michael clapped his hands. "Okay, back to business." He waved his hand toward the library and said, "Come on Josh, let's see if I can find it. Then we can watch some playoff baseball on the big screen. Big game tonight!" The two walked into Michael's elaborate study that held hundreds of books. He walked over to a shelf and found a Bible.

"I have it marked here. Let's take a look. Yes, here it is. 'Do not store treasures for yourself here on earth where it can be destroyed by rust and moths, or where thieves can steal them. Instead, store up your treasures in heaven where they cannot be touched by rust or moths, or stolen by thieves. For wherever your treasure is, that is where your heart will be, too.' Pretty powerful, huh?"

Josh looked puzzled.

"What are you thinking, Josh?" Michael asked.

"Okay, I don't mean to be disrespectful but, first, yes, it is very interesting. But I can't help but notice. You have a ten million dollar house here, another back in New York, you've got, what, half a million dollars in cars at your two houses, and a boat that had to have cost a couple million, at least...."

"Five. Plus tax," Michael admitted.

"You're making my case for me, Grandpa. With all due respect, and I am not judging you at all, but it seems like you have, as Jesus said, a lot of stuff stored up here for rust and thieves."

"You make a valid point, and a natural one, I would think. But I think you miss the ultimate point."

"What's that?"

"Jesus wasn't saying people shouldn't have stuff. In fact, many of the most famous figures in the Bible were wealthy: Abraham, David, Solomon. Wealth isn't what is bad; a stray heart is what is bad. Now, the point Jesus was making there is that if your focus is on the material things, then it will pull your heart in the wrong direction. That is why we have to be vigilant. If it were impossible to have a good heart while having stuff, then only the poorest people in the world would be able to have good hearts. Here is what I have found: There are poor people with good hearts and poor people with bad hearts. There are rich people with good hearts and rich people with bad hearts. Stuff isn't the problem. The state of the heart is the issue."

"So how does that work with you and all your stuff?"

"I will be honest and say that it is definitely a distraction to have so much stuff. So the point is well-taken. There is so much effort just to take care of it all. It takes a lot of time just fixing things when they break. Granted, I am in a position to pay others to do the work, but I have to manage them. It takes a lot of focus."

"So why do you do it?"

"We can afford it. That isn't a problem. Ultimately, we enjoy it. But I recognize the issue and work extra to make sure that the material things don't put the squeeze on my heart. I think the big thing I have learned is that I choose where I will put my focus. The key thing I try to remember is the last part: For wherever your treasure is, that is where your heart will be, too.

"I constantly ask myself where I am placing my treasure. Both the literal and the figurative treasure. And where I put my treasure is where my heart will naturally go."

"What do you mean literally and figuratively?"

"Well, literally, if I just keep buying more and more stuff endlessly, then my heart and focus will go to the stuff. I spent a month looking for and studying that fishing boat. That was a month of focus. Now I spend a considerable amount of time every month keeping it up. Again, I don't do it, but I have to make sure it gets done. And it is a distraction. All the more reason I have to make sure I keep my heart focused on what is right.

"As for the figurative, there are all sorts of things that can steal our heart's focus. Those are the foes, which we can talk about later. Some of them are seemingly good but can pull us away. Wealth, fame, success, etc...."

"So, Grandpa, what did you start doing to focus your heart? What did you call them? Disciplines?"

"That's right. I have to discipline my life to make room for my heart to constantly grow. That's how I foster it." Michael looked at the clock and saw that the baseball game was about to start. "What do you say we continue this tomorrow and go watch the playoff game?"

"Sounds like a deal." With that, they headed off to watch the game in the plush theater Michael had built just for such occasions as this.

Later that night, as Michael and Amy were lying in bed before going to sleep, they reflected on their lives and their relationships with their children and grandchildren.

"You know," Michael said, "it sure is fun to spend some time with Josh. I wish I would have done more of that over the years. It just seems like I spent so much time working."

"It is true what they say, 'They grow up fast.'"

"I feel a little guilty, actually," Michael lamented.

"How so?"

"I just think about how fortunate I was to learn the Twelve Pillars and how they changed my life, and then I spent so little time passing them on. I applied them to my own life with such great success, but not so much time passing them on to others, even my family."

"But you are teaching them to Josh now, along with other lessons you have learned."

"I suppose. I should focus on that as the good thing. I need to make an effort now, though, to make sure that I spend more time with the kids and grandkids so I can teach them these things."

"That's a good idea, Michael. When Josh goes home, let's sit down over the calendar and make sure we get some visits on the schedule."

"Great idea. Let's do it." Michael just stared up at the ceiling until his eyes closed softly and he drifted into sleep.

When she realized Michael had fallen asleep, she kissed him lightly on the cheek. "Night-night," she said, as she rolled over to go to sleep herself.

CHAPTER

V

• • • •

The next morning, after sleeping in, Michael suggested to Amy and Josh that the three of them take a drive through Ding Darling National Wildlife Refuge. Ding Darling was named in honor of the conservationist who encouraged President Harry Truman to set aside some 6,400 acres of Sanibel Island as a wildlife refuge. Michael loved to drive through the refuge to see the many birds and alligators that live there among the marshes and mangroves. He often went there alone, and of course with Amy and the many people who came to the island to visit them.

After driving into the refuge, they found a spot with an overlook of a marsh. There were some cormorants off to one side, their wings spread out to let them dry in the warmth of the sun. In the distance, they could see two alligators also sunning, just out of the water. There were hardly any other people there at the refuge at that moment, and it was eerily quiet.

"I sure love this place," Michael said. "Even though it is so simple and hardly ever changes, it is a place that brings me peace."

"I am guessing this is the segue to our discussion of fostering your heart?" Josh asked.

"It is as good a place as any," Michael responded.

Josh pulled out his recorder and held it up. "I figured that might be the case, so I brought this." He hit the record button and stuck it in his shirt pocket. "Ready."

"Well, Josh, as I said, I realized that I hadn't taken time to foster my heart. I had gotten so caught up in business and life that I forgot to tend to my soul.

That's when I started learning about the disciplines. You see, most of life just happens. But the good stuff doesn't seem to just happen. You have to make it happen. You have to discipline yourself to make it happen."

"Like, what do you mean?"

"It would probably be good to talk a little about the foes of the heart, because they are things that just happen. I really believe that people today have a much harder time fostering their heart because of how fast-paced life is nowadays. Think about it. A hundred and fifty years ago, life was much more peaceful. Don't get me wrong, I am glad we live now. Over my lifetime, we have seen the greatest advances in human history—medical, technological, and scientific advances previous generations only dreamed of. But it has come at a cost to the heart, I believe."

"How so?" Josh asked.

"All of the noise, all of the decisions, all of the travel and movement. The hustle and bustle of everyday life. It all keeps us busy, so we never spend time alone with ourselves, with our thoughts. Technology, materialism, and the like, all war against our hearts. These are the foes of the heart. They tend to keep us outwardly focused rather than inwardly focused."

"So, are you saying that technology is bad?"

"No, not at all. I love technology. It is just that technology does nothing to foster my heart. Technology is utilitarian. It is a tool to be used. But most of it, by its nature, dehumanizes. Televisions keep people from talking or thinking, as do personal music players. People shut off from themselves and others. It is great that we can watch a ballgame or an educational show, or get the nightly news of what is going on in the world, but we cannot let technology rule our lives. It can become a foe because it crowds out the heart."

There was a walking path just a few hundred feet down the road. Michael suggested they take a walk deeper into the refuge. As they walked, he continued.

"When I realized that all of the noise of life and all of the sensations were part of my problem, I resolved to discipline myself to take control of my heart by doing things that would let it grow and become that foundation—that wellspring—which would allow me to experience true success. I knew if I didn't, I would crash and burn eventually. So, I began with the disciplines, implementing them into my life."

"What are the disciplines?"

Just then a bald eagle flew overhead. Amy pointed. "Look, guys. Isn't it beautiful?"

"It sure is. Look at it just glide," Michael said. After watching it a few moments, Michael went back to the question. "The disciplines, yes. Well, there are five I have practiced over the years, some better than others, and some with more effectiveness than others. I truly had to discipline myself to practice them."

"What are they?"

"The first is solitude. I realized that I never had time to myself. I was always with other people. With Amy and your dad and Aunt Jennifer. Then off to work to be with all the people there, going to meetings and making and taking calls all day. Then off to be with people at night at various functions. It was overwhelming. I knew that I needed to take time for myself. So, I began to discipline myself to do it. I began getting up a half-hour earlier and would go down to my study to just be alone. I used to take two weekends a year and go somewhere, mainly to retreat centers, and just be alone. It was such an amazing breakthrough for me. It actually made me better."

"Better? How?"

"It made me more peaceful. It made me a better husband and father. It made me a better boss and businessman. You know, Albert Einstein said that the monotony of solitude actually stimulates the creative mind. Thomas Merton said that it was in solitude that he found the gentleness with which to love others. And that was my experience as well." After a moment of pause, he continued. "You know, some of the loneliest times of my life have been in a crowd of people. And some of the most satisfying, peaceful, and fulfilling moments of my life have been when I was alone."

"How can you be lonely when you are with people?"

"The heart needs connection with others, Josh. Just because you are with people doesn't mean you are connected to people. You can be in a very large crowd, and if you don't know anyone and can't connect with them, you can feel lonely. And the opposite is true. You can be with no one else, entirely alone, and feel a total sense of connection and peace."

"So you just go and hang out by yourself? That sounds extremely boring. How would that help you?"

"Mainly because of the next three things on my list, which I was able to do uninterrupted because I was alone."

"Oh, look at the fish jump," Josh exclaimed, pointing behind his grandma and grandpa. There were some fish jumping out of the water.

"Yes, look at that," Michael said. "The three things," he continued. "First, is silence. That rich king, Solomon, also taught that there is a time to speak and a time to be silent. Unfortunately, we have mastered the speaking part and forgotten the power of silence. Utter, blissful silence. Do you know how much you can hear when you are alone and silent?"

"Uh, no. How can you hear when it is silent? Aren't they in opposition to each other?"

"Not at all, Josh. In fact, I can hear best when I am alone and in silence. I can hear my heart. I can hear my thoughts and feelings. I can hear the words of others that I can finally spend some time pondering. Life is so fast when we are in our daily routine, and there is so much being said to us all the time, that when we get alone, and when we take away all the chatter, we can finally actually connect with all that is inside of us.

"I would take my journal with me and just write down all the thoughts that came to my mind that I wanted to think deeply about and ponder. It was interesting to me how, when I first started doing it, that it took a while for me to settle down and learn to cut through all the noise inside of me and listen to my heart. At first, I would be so antsy. There would just be so much flooding my mind. But as I persevered, staying in silence, gradually it all sorted out. And that allowed me to really see inside of myself. The self I wasn't able to connect with because of how busy I was during the regular time of my life, I was now alone with, and able to hear like I could not otherwise hear.

"Mother Teresa used to talk about how the trees, flowers, and grass all grew in silence and how the sun, moon, and stars all moved in the silence. She said that we ourselves needed the silence to be able to touch the souls—the hearts—of others. It was in the times of silence that I grew, that I found my strength that allowed me to be the man I needed to be for my family and for my growing business."

"I don't really like being alone, or being quiet for that matter. I think it would drive me crazy," Josh noted.

"It does take some getting used to. And, yes, it can be intimidating at first. It's surprising really, that we are so often more comfortable being with others than being with ourselves. But for the sake of your paper on what made me successful, I would be remiss to not talk about the practice of silence."

"So how long would you go without talking or without any other noise?"

"Well, sometimes a couple of days. It's hard to crowd out all noise. The sound you make just living you can't get rid of. The sound of nature I never counted as noise. You know, birds, the wind blowing through the trees. Rain." At that, Michael suggested they turn back to the car.

"So what is the second thing you did when you were alone?"

"The second thing I did when I would be in solitude was to read. Reading is one of the primary ways to foster your heart. Do you know the name Victor Hugo?"

"Sure, the French poet. I learned about him last year in school."

"One of my favorite quotes about reading was from Hugo. He said that to learn to read is to light a fire. Every syllable was a spark. Profound. That's how it was with me. I would always have a few books with me when I was alone."

"What kind of books?"

"Good question. There was a certain kind of book that I read when I was alone. I didn't read business books or anything like that. When I was purposefully alone, I would always take books that would touch my heart. Books of poetry, meditation. Deep, profound things. Never pop culture kinds of books. Literature. Josh, we have, I believe, lost our depth as people. You don't meet many deep people anymore. Too many people today are a mile wide and an inch deep. This kind of reading made my well—to get back to our analogy—deeper. That way, I could draw from the depths of my heart when I needed it. People who don't read do not achieve the depth that they need to draw from."

"Is that it? Those are the only kinds of books you read?"

"Occasionally, I would bring a biography of a great person. Someone I could learn from, who would open my mind. Someone who was a deeper person than I was. The whole idea was to take me deeper and to strengthen my heart. Ultimately, reading allows me to meet new people, to hear new thoughts, to travel to new lands, and to cross the boundaries of time. Reading allows me to control what I hear and how fast I hear it. Many times, I would read something and then close the book and just think about what I had just read. That was where my heart would reap the reward. You know, where else but with reading can you meet someone from today or the past whom you would never be able to spend time with, and learn from their wisdom and experience?"

"Good point. Sometimes it is boring, though."

"Yes, sometimes it is boring. But if it is too hard to get through something, find something else that you can get through. Something that touches your heart. Beyond that, though, I think a lot of people have gotten lazy with how visual our culture has become. They want to watch something rather than read about something. They want to see someone else's picture of a sunset rather than see or imagine it for themselves. I think a lot of people would do well to train themselves to read more. I found it powerful to spend time alone with some books. That is definitely part of the secret to my success."

"Okay, what about the last one?"

"It isn't the last one. There is one more after this next one, but this is the last one that I practiced in solitude."

"That's right. That's what I meant."

"Prayer is next. Now, I know there are lots of different views on prayer and there have been tens of thousands of books written on it, so I am not going to get into a theological discussion, but rather, my own simple explanation. Prayer, to me, is simply the act of communing and talking with God. Do you pray, Josh?"

"Sure, I pray. You know, when I need stuff I ask God to help."

"That's good, but I am talking about something deeper than that. I am talking about finding that time of communion and transcendence that allows your heart to grow. I believe that we are all designed to live eternally and transcend this world. There is a part of us, deep in there somewhere— and don't ask me where—that transcends this world."

"So what do you do when you pray?"

"The old Quakers had a concept of 'centering down.' It was essentially finding your center through prayer and communing with God. Combined with being alone and being in silence, I could pray. It was there that I could take my concerns and worries and fears and release them. I could find the negative aspects of my heart and character and let them go. The time I had to find my true inner heart and then to give that over to God was priceless in my success."

"So it is basically talking with God."

"No, I would put it differently. I would say that prayer is not talking to God, but rather being with God."

"Being with God?"

"Yes, exactly. You know, I am obviously not a Hindu, but Gandhi said something that made a lot of sense to me about prayer."

"What was that?"

"He said that it was better to have a heart without words than to have words without a heart. To me, God is interested in our hearts, not our words. And so, when I pray, sometimes I use words and other times I don't. But in it all, I try to make my heart accessible so that God can change it."

Amy jumped in. "You know, Josh, Martin Luther, who started the Reformation, prayed a prayer that I often recite. 'Grant that I may not pray alone with the mouth, but help me that I may pray from the depths of my heart.'"

"That's a good one," Michael added.

They were almost back to the car so Josh asked about the final discipline that his grandfather practiced to foster his heart.

"The last one is my least favorite, but it sure was good for my heart when I did it. It was certainly the most difficult. The last discipline is fasting."

"Fasting? What's that?"

"Fasting means not eating."

"Count me out!" Josh said.

Michael and Amy laughed out loud. "It isn't so bad. You know, you do it every day."

"Huh?"

"Sure, that's where we get the word 'breakfast.' We break our fast. You regularly go from five or six at night until seven or eight the next morning without food. That's up to fifteen hours. So when you wake up, you break that fast by eating. But when you fast like I am talking about, you do it purposefully and for a longer period of time."

"What good could possibly come from fasting?"

"You know, fasting has been around for a long time, in both the religious world and outside of religion. There are lots of thoughts on the benefits of it, but there was one single reason that always made it worthwhile for me."

"What's that?"

"Fasting showed me the depth of rationalization that my heart could achieve, and in turn, fasting strengthened my will and resolve to know what was right and stick by it, no matter what the circumstances. Most people are unaware of their ability to rationalize and deceive themselves."

"How in the world does not eating help you with that?"

"It is simple, really. I would decide to fast for a time, say three days, and away I went. Soon enough, the hunger would become unbearable and my heart would begin to rationalize things. I would find myself making all sorts of excuses for why I didn't need to fast. I would be having this internal argument going on. I was on one side, and then I was on the other. It became clear to me that this happens all the time. Our hearts crumble and we rationalize when something gets hard. We make excuses and can even deceive ourselves because it gets hard and we want out. Fasting taught me to not listen to that internal rationalization. I would make all kinds of excuses to myself to allow myself to eat.

"Well, there were times in my life I was tempted to make all kinds of excuses to make money or grow my business. After making it through a fast, my heart was stronger and I was more aware to be able to handle the daily world around me and the challenges it presents.

"Frankly, I don't know on a deep level exactly why it works, or how. I just know that it does. One other thing that fasting does is that it brings clarity to my thinking. When you are alone, and quiet, and prayerful, and then to top it all off, you haven't eaten, your senses are extraordinarily heightened. I am able to think more clearly. I get answers more clearly to the things I am thinking about."

"Interesting." Josh was pondering it all. It was certainly above the depth of much of what he had thought about before. And it was far beyond what he thought his grandpa would tell him was the secret to his success. He thought Michael would talk about hard work, perseverance, risk-taking, and the importance of timing. Never in a million years did he think he would get answers like he was hearing.

They reached the car and got in. Michael turned on the air conditioning, as it was getting pretty warm out. "Let's suspend the conversation about me for the rest of the tour. Instead, let's just enjoy the beauty of this fabulous place."

"Sounds like a deal, Grandpa. I am just trying to digest it all anyway." Josh turned the recorder off.

They spent the next forty-five minutes driving slowly through Ding Darling, occasionally getting out to walk closer to the wildlife and look into the water. Just two grandparents and their oldest grandchild, mostly silent, enjoying the wonder of nature. When they got home, they ordered a pizza from the local delivery joint and spent a quiet evening at home.

The next morning Michael, Amy, and Josh all got up and went to spend the morning and early afternoon on Second Chance. They spent some time fishing, and a little bit of time talking about Michael's life. Josh wanted to make sure he got all of the actual details of Michael's business life and the growth of his retail chain. Michael also filled him in some on the many philanthropic endeavors he and Amy were involved in.

As they neared the end of the boat trip, Michael realized that there were still many things he wanted to share with Josh about the issues of the heart. "You know, Josh, we aren't going to have time for me to tell you all the things I want to tell you that I have learned about guarding your heart. I guess we shouldn't have spent so much time fishing and watching baseball."

"But it was fun," Josh replied.

"It sure was. Hey, I have an idea. How about I write some ideas up and e-mail them to you so you can use them in your report?"

"Sure, what kind of stuff?"

"Well, I have been thinking about how, in many areas, there are two contrasting sides that try to take control of your heart. And usually, whichever one gains control, it just goes from there. There is a battle for the control of our hearts. Almost like two teams competing."

"What do you mean, Grandpa?"

"For instance, greed and generosity. Both are issues of the heart. Whichever one you allow to take root, whichever one takes control, is the direction you tend to go."

"That's an easy one," Josh noted. "Just like hockey."

"Huh?" Michael was lost.

"Oh, sorry, Grandpa. I mean the alliteration. Face-offs. Just like in hockey. You start with neutrality and you have a face-off. The battle for control. That's the start."

"Perfect example, Josh! So where does that leave us? Focus. Foes. Foster. And now face-offs. I'll tell you what. Give me a week, and I will get you a list of the face-offs I've experienced. I will write up some thoughts and you can use them for your project. That sound like a deal?"

"Okay, Grandpa. Deal. You can have two weeks if you need it."

"Thanks, buddy." He rubbed his hand quickly back and forth through Josh's short hair. "You're the best. Now, let's get one more round of fishing in."

Early that evening, Michael and Amy took Josh back to Southwest Florida International Airport in Fort Myers so he could catch his plane back home. They waited until the last moment they could to send him through the security line by himself, before they gave him their hugs and kisses so he could be on his way.

VI

. . . .

T wo weeks had gone by, and Michael had spent many hours typing his thoughts about the struggles of the heart that he and others had gone through—the "face-offs," as Josh had dubbed them. He reflected deeply on how they had affected him personally over the years. Now, after getting it all down on his word-processing program, Michael typed a brief note to Josh, cut and pasted it into his e-mail program, and pressed "Send."

Dear Josh,

Your grandmother and I were so happy to have you down to visit us a couple of weekends ago. You are growing up into such a fine young man, and we enjoyed our time together. We are very proud of you.

As promised, I have written some of my thoughts on some of the "face-offs" that we are confronted with. I have peppered my thoughts with some pertinent quotes that have caused me to think over the years. I have tried to give you real-life examples and not just stay in the realm of the theoretical. I personally liked giving this some thought over the past few weeks and believe that it has helped me as much as it will you. It is always good to go over important truths again and again. G.K. Chesterton once said that we needed to be "reminded more than instructed." I believe that to be wholly true.

Here they are, in no particular order, other than that is how I thought of them.

SEVEN FACE-OFFS OF THE HEART

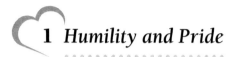

1 *Humility and Pride*

A t the deepest levels of our heart, we are either humble or proud, and that makes all the difference in the world. When I say "pride" I do not mean the positive use of the word as in "take pride in your work." That kind of pride is not only good, but admirable. No, the pride I speak of is that deep root that considers itself better than others, can never be wrong, and seeks its own glory. It causes us to seek our own interests rather than the interests of others. It is concerned only with the increase of self.

Pride can be deceptive. One can appear humble and yet be proud. One can be proud of how humble they are, and in doing so, defy the existence of their humility.

Pride is concerned with how it is perceived and viewed. It has to always win. It can never say "I'm sorry" or "I was wrong." Pride puts others down and tries to build itself up. In the end, Solomon was right in his proverb that said, "Pride comes before a fall."

There were times in my life after I got successful that I really struggled with pride. I forgot that I was someone who, through happenstance, learned some lessons from someone else that enabled me to become successful. I began to think that I was something special. And the more financially successful I became, the more other people confirmed for me how "special" I was. I began to hold myself in high regard and others with disregard. Eventually, I began to have problems with relationships. People don't do business with proud, arrogant people.

I remember one instance, right after things started taking off, when I got into a disagreement with a vendor of mine. Deep down, I knew he was right, but I couldn't let it go. I had to be right—or so I thought—in order to make sure that he understood how strong I was. I didn't want him thinking I was weak and then taking advantage of me in the future. Eventually, I realized that he was going to stop doing business with me if I didn't relent. I had to swallow my pride and make amends. When I did, it set the relationship right and we have made each other millions of dollars since. After that, I began to really think about my need to be truly humble.

Saint Augustine said, "Humility is the foundation of all the other virtues, hence, in the soul in which this virtue does not exist, there cannot be any other virtue except in mere appearance." How true. If we don't have humility, we cannot have other virtues. We may appear to have others, but it will be in appearance only.

So, what is humility? Is it being weak, or letting people run roughshod over us? No, I do not believe that it is. Does it mean that we are always wrong or that we must let everyone have their way? Does it mean not standing up for yourself? Again, no. I like what Charles Spurgeon said: "Humility is to make a right estimate of one's self."

I found that both ends of the spectrum need humility. The rich can be tempted to say that they are better than the poor because of their success and wealth, while the poor can be tempted to be proud that they haven't "sold out" for money. We need humility to understand that we all make choices in life. We make different choices, and that is okay.

Humility is knowing that we are better than no one and that we are no worse than anyone. Each and every individual has an innate value and worth. Letting that be the core of your heart and living that out is what allows us to think rightly about ourselves. It will keep us from the kind of dangers that befall those who consider themselves greater than they ought to.

In life, choose humility, Josh. Swallow your pride. Put it out of your heart. Do not let it take root. How can we do that? A couple of things have been helpful to me. First, look at yourself with sober reality. Don't overplay your strengths and underplay your weaknesses. Second, view the world with appreciation.

Humility is to see ourselves in reality, not in our lofty perceptions or in the perceptions others have of us. It is to recognize our place here in humanity, that no one is any better than anyone else.

Benjamin Franklin said, "Humility makes great men twice honorable." To live with honor, live with humility.

2 *Forgiveness and Retribution*

There is a truth that is undeniable. If you live here on earth and you interact with anyone else, eventually, someone will wrong you. Your parents will wrong you. Your siblings will wrong you. Your spouse will wrong you. Your children will wrong you. Your friends will wrong you. Your neighbors will wrong you. Your co-workers will wrong you. And here is the truth that stands it all on its head: You will also wrong them. Once you accept these facts, you are in a positive position to deal with that grim aspect of life.

Forgiveness is not a display of weakness. It is the ultimate act of strength. Only the strong and secure in heart can forgive. Weak people hold grudges and seek retribution. Forgiveness brings people together, while retribution drives them apart.

The most ironic aspect of an unforgiving heart is that the one it really hurts the most is the one who will not forgive. Lewis Smedes says, "To forgive is to set a prisoner free and discover that the prisoner was you." Early on, I had a real problem with forgiveness. When someone would wrong me, I would try to wrong them back. Then I realized the foolishness of that. This actually only made it worse for me because it drove my lack of forgiveness "underground," so to speak. Now, I wouldn't actively seek retribution, but I did hold it in my heart. It ate away at me and was like a weed that grew.

Smedes was right in that I was the one who was held prisoner when I didn't forgive. There were times that someone would wrong me and they didn't even know it. They went on about their lives, and I was the one who suffered internally by holding it all inside rather than releasing forgiveness.

To allow yourself to hold on to a heart of retribution—whether or not you actually seek retribution—will slowly kill your heart. Your heart will become hard. You will become suspicious of others. You will have a difficult time enjoying life. Your bitterness will wear itself on your face. I see people all the time who look like they just sucked on a lemon. When you get to know them, you see they are angry from their lack of a forgiving heart. Life for them is a succession of beating others. Everyone is their enemy. This is no way to live.

Imagine what the world would be like if everyone would forgive. I love what Mark Twain said: "Forgiveness is the fragrance that the violet sheds on the heel that has crushed it." Even when something goes wrong or someone doesn't treat you right, your choice of whether to forgive or seek retribution is what will determine how the situation goes forward. Will it escalate? Or will you seek to turn it around and use the situation to learn and grow together? The choice is ours alone.

One last thought about forgiveness. "He who is devoid of the power to forgive, is devoid of the power to love." This is from Martin Luther King Jr. The greatest act of humanity is to love, and without forgiveness, we cannot truly love. Someday you will get married, Josh, and that woman who takes your breath away will also drive you crazy at times—as you will her. Living in close proximity will do that to people. Yet, you will have stood before God and witnesses and promised to love her. You cannot love her if you will not forgive her. To keep a heart pure, we must continually forgive our spouses, our families, and those around us.

3 Vulnerability and Protectiveness

I have met many people throughout the years who say, "I am never going to be hurt again." They have had a bad experience, someone wronged them, and they have vowed to make sure that it happens no more. Unfortunately, the person who suffers is them. You cannot keep people from hurting you. It is a part of life. What makes the difference is how you respond.

The word "vulnerability" comes from the Latin word that means "to wound." To allow yourself to be open to being wounded is the only way to build relationships that will help you enjoy your success. You see, the good comes with the bad. To live in relationship with people means you have to stay close enough to them where they can do you either harm or good. If you are distanced so much that they can't do you harm, they cannot do you good either. That decision is made in the heart.

M. Scott Peck said that "there can be no community without vulnerability." To live in community is to place ourselves willingly into proximity with others. And that leaves us open, both figuratively and literally, to be hurt.

Vulnerability is the risk we take in order to experience the vastness of love. We can either love fully, and risk being harmed, or we can decide that we will close off our hearts and, thus, close off our opportunity to love and be loved.

I had been hurt a number of times both in my personal life and in business. I decided that I would just close myself off from others. In the end, that did me no good. I became very lonely and sad because I had no authentic and deep relationships. I had relationships, but they all stayed at the surface. I didn't want anyone to know me because I was afraid that if they knew me they would possibly reject me. I was afraid that if I developed a relationship with people and those relationships went bad, I would just suffer more than if I kept everything at the lowest level.

What happened was that I ended up with no one to talk to, no one to share things with. In order to protect myself from relational harm, I had done something that actually *caused* me relational harm. I had to undo that.

I began to reach out to others. I began to allow others to see my weaknesses. You know, as my net worth grew and I ended up on the covers of magazines and gained national notoriety, people began to assume I was some sort of "superhuman." I started out behind the eight ball in terms of developing relationships with people because of their perceptions of me. I had to proactively open myself up to being known.

I made a commitment to not protect myself so much. This doesn't mean that I ran around baring my soul to anyone who would listen. This was purposeful, proactive vulnerability with people I knew I could develop a long-term, mutually beneficial friendship or business relationship with.

As I did this, I noticed that others did as well. I got to know others much better than I ever had before. I had much better give-and-take with people. I developed some very close friends who became a source of strength when I had rough times. In good times, we were able to enjoy them together.

My encouragement to you, Josh, is to not wall yourself off from other people in order to protect yourself. Let others in. Will some people hurt you? Yes. But the pain some cause will be more than made up for by those positive relationships you establish with those you can be vulnerable with and allow into your heart.

Madeleine L'Engle rightly said that "when we were children, we used to think that when we were grown-up we would no longer be vulnerable. But to grow up is to accept vulnerability.... To be alive is to be vulnerable." Wise words.

4 *Courage and Fear*

Over the years, I have sought the answer to a simple question: Why is it that some people achieve success while others fail? The answers to that question are profound. One of the simplest answers is that those who have hearts filled with courage succeed, while those who live in fear fail.

I have met many very successful people in my career, people worth billions and people who have built terrific small businesses—successful, every one of them. I have met Olympic athletes and high-achieving people in so many different fields. And do you know one common trait amongst all of them? Fear. I myself feel fear all the time. What separates the successful from the unsuccessful? It isn't that the successful have no fear. Everyone experiences fear. The successful do two things. First, they cultivate a heart of courage. Second, they act on courage rather than fear. Mark Twain said, "Courage is resistance to fear, mastery of fear—not absence of fear." When we are confronted with an action or situation that causes us fear, we have a choice: Face the fear head-on, and take the appropriate action, or fall back in fear and inaction. Will we become masters of or slaves to fear?

I have found that anything of worth requires courage. Aristotle said, "You will never do anything in this world without courage." It's true. One can be afraid of almost anything. When playing sports in high school, you can be afraid of your opponent. When in college, you can be afraid that you won't do well. When you graduate, you can be afraid you won't find a job. When you buy your first house, you can be afraid you won't be able to make the payments. When you have children, you can be afraid that they won't turn out to be productive members of society. As you age, you can be afraid of health problems. A person with fear in his or her heart will always find something to be afraid of in any situation.

All of the good things in life will require you to make a decision: Will you be fearful or show courage?

Some people are afraid of what others will think of them. I remember when I started to become successful, some of the people closest to me started to resent me. One of my favorite writers over the years has been Ralph Waldo Emerson. I found this a while back, and it is good advice: "Whatever course you decide upon, there is always someone to tell you that you are wrong. There are always difficulties arising which tempt you to believe that your critics are right. To map out a course of action and follow it to an end requires courage." There will always be people who will second-guess your decisions. Most of them do so because they don't have the courage to make the same decision. It will require courage for you to forge ahead.

Ultimately, fear or courage is simply a state that we choose. Napoleon Hill said, "Fears are nothing more than a state of mind." We will dwell on one or the other. We will act on one or the other. The final decision will be whether we have the will to make the right—the courageous—decision. The only way to ensure that we do is to guard our heart so that it is filled with courage and strong enough to do the right thing when the time comes.

One of the books that the old maintenance man on the Twelve Pillars estate told me to read was by one of the great self-help writers of all time, Dale Carnegie. It was called *How to Win Friends and Influence People*. It is a classic. That got me to reading his other works. A couple of things he said have challenged me through the years to make sure I always take courageous action:

"Action breeds confidence and courage. If you want to conquer fear, do not sit home and think about it. Go out and get busy.

"Inaction breeds doubt and fear. Do the thing you fear to do and keep on doing it.... That is the quickest and surest way ever yet discovered to conquer fear."

I have always liked that. If you take action, you produce courage. If you don't act, you produce fear. When you act in spite of fear and achieve success, it helps eliminate future fear because you now have a past victory over fear that will give you courage for the future. Good words to remember, Josh.

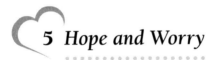

5 Hope and Worry

This is an expansion on courage and fear. One of the things I became aware of early on in my transformation was the understanding of how our minds work in the projection of the future. You see, you mostly experience courage and fear in the moment, though you can have courage and fear about the future. Hope and worry, however, are almost exclusively in the realm of the future. We either hope the future will be better or we worry that it will be worse.

Now, here is where it gets interesting. If that is true, then hope and worry are acts of the imagination, which is an aspect of the heart. We cannot *know* the future. We can only *imagine* the future. Think about how this works for or against us.

The future is going to be what it is going to be. Yes, we work hard to shape our future and make it work the way we want it to work, but there are so many things out of our control that we cannot determine our future. We can only shape and steer it.

So, whether we worry or have hope, what is going to happen is going to happen. In the meantime, we live in either a positive or negative state. I found that life happened whether I worried or not. So I decided to stop worrying because it was eating away at me from the inside.

The other thing I noticed with worry and hope was that, to a certain degree, they became self-fulfilling. When I would worry, it would put me in a negative state and I wouldn't perform as well. I would react negatively. I would make more mistakes. What I worried about was more likely to come true. And the opposite was true as well. If I focused my heart on what I hoped for, I was in a positive state and I performed at a higher level. The state of my heart truly was the wellspring of life. It brought forward both positive and negative things, depending on where my focus was. Goethe was right when he said, "It is better to hope than despair."

So, I began to make my philosophy be like what Einstein said: "Learn from yesterday, live for today, hope for tomorrow." I let go of yesterday and didn't worry about it. I took each day at a time and did the absolute best I could. And when I thought of tomorrow, I forced myself to look at it from a positive perspective of hope. It became such a benefit to me every day to keep my heart focused in a positive direction.

What about when things are going poorly and look like they will become even worse? That is a good question. I am not suggesting we live in a fantasyland. There will be times when things go wrong and look like they will continue to. What then? Well, we still have a choice about what our focus can be. We can recognize the challenges we face and still be hopeful that things will turn out well. Even when we have lost hope, we can choose to act hopefully. Dale Carnegie reminded us that "most of the important things in the world have been accomplished by people who have kept on

trying when there seemed to be no hope at all." Almost every person I
ever met who accomplished great things did so in the face of adversity and
obstacles. They may have come to the end of their hope, and still, they acted
on the hope that, if they kept trying, one more day or one more week, they
would eventually succeed.

Ultimately, hope and worry are about the quality of our lives. Maya
Angelou, the famous poet, said, "We spend precious hours fearing
the inevitable. It would be wise to use that time adoring our families,
cherishing our friends, and living our lives." Each and every day, we have
only twenty-four hours. We make a decision about where our hearts will
lie that day. I made the choice to enjoy my family, my friends, and my life. I
would encourage you to do the same.

I feel sorry for those who fall into the cycle of worry. They live in a prison
of their own making. They most often suffer the "torments of grief... from
the evil which never arrived," as Emerson said. Josh, guard your heart from
worry. Do not be overly concerned. Tomorrow will come and you can deal
with it then. Do your best today, prepare for tomorrow, and keep your heart
filled with hope.

6 *Generosity and Greed*

. . . .

Josh, one of the travesties of our time is that, in the midst of the greatest expansion and advancement in human history, we still suffer from the battle between generosity and greed. Some would say that greed drove that advancement and brought us the world we enjoy. I would disagree with that. Certainly, people who push society forward enjoy the rewards. But I don't believe that many greedy people actually make much of themselves in the long run. And even if they do succeed at storing up a pile of money, I don't see how they can enjoy it if their hearts aren't generous.

Horace said, "He who is greedy is always in want." A famous American billionaire was once asked, "How much money is enough?" to which he replied, "Just a little bit more." The Bible says whoever loves money never has money enough. That has been stated many other ways by many other people. Greed is something that wraps its tentacles around our heart and squeezes the life out of it.

I have found that greed stems from a few different places.

It comes from pride (you will note that lots of these qualities I am writing to you about overlap). People want more because it makes them feel successful. Their identity is wrapped up in the accomplishment of getting more. Theirs is a "top of the heap" mentality—the "whoever dies with the most toys, wins" ideology. Neither produces success that is enjoyable. It is a treadmill one can never get off. There will always be someone with more.

It comes from fear. People who are afraid of not having enough become greedy. Their focus becomes on having, rather than being. They place their own needs in front of others. They store up for themselves so they can feel secure. Josh, there is no security in life. Billions of dollars can go away fast, let alone the money of an average person. We should work to make ourselves secure and take care of our families, but we cannot become greedy in doing so. Greed robs us of joy.

Greed comes from a skewed perspective of the eternal nature of mankind. People think that if they can possess, they can stake their place here on earth. They forget that we are here just for a short while, and then we pass on. Nothing we do can keep us here. The great theologian A.W. Tozer wrote: "There is within the human heart a tough fibrous root of fallen life whose nature is to possess, always to possess. It covets 'things' with a deep and fierce passion." Our mistake is thinking that to possess will somehow keep us from having to move on. We all die. We all lose everything that we have come to possess.

Generosity is the antidote to greed. It is a choice we make. Will we allow our hearts to be focused on what we want and what we can get? Or will we recognize the temporal aspect of money and possessions and be generous people? What would happen if we held—figuratively speaking—all of our money and possessions in an open hand? How would our lives change if we were generous in heart and not greedy? How would the world change?

This is not about money, by the way. There are misconceptions that the "rich" are greedy and the poor are generous. Or that the only way to be generous is to have wealth. These are all misconceptions. Here is what I know. I have met greedy poor people and greedy rich people. I have met generous poor people and generous rich people. It isn't about how much money you have or your place in life. It is always about your heart. I remember once in one of our stores, there was a cleaning lady who would come in after the store was closed for the day. One of our other employees was having some financial problems, and I found out that this cleaning lady, who didn't make much money at all, had given the other employee a significant amount of money to help with the situation. That had a profound impact on me. To see someone with so little, give so much. It was a heart of generosity. And I have seen wealthy people who could make a difference, who will give some money in token amounts, but are not particularly generous.

Some people wonder how they can be generous if they don't have much. I like what Mother Teresa's advice was. "If you can't feed a hundred people, then just feed one." Some have resources to make a large impact, while others have only enough resources to make a small impact. The key is to make an impact.

You may wonder, and others have as well, how one can get ahead if they are giving all the time. There is the thought that if you give it away, it is gone, but this is not true. It actually works the other way. It is a spiritual law. You reap what you sow. Buddha gave a great analogy: "Thousands of candles can be lit from a single candle, and the life of the candle will not be shortened. Happiness never decreases by being shared."

The power of generosity affects both you and others. When we give to someone else, it is easy to see how they can have joy in receiving. Someone in need feels good when their need is met. But what many people do not realize is that there is joy for the one who does the giving, oftentimes more joy than the one who is receiving. One thing I got into the habit of doing was giving my cars away to overseas relief workers and medical missionaries. I would pay to have the cars shipped overseas so they could have dependable transportation in rural places where the trip to the doctor can be four hundred miles or more.

Now, when I buy a new car, I enjoy it. I like new cars. But when they are a couple of years old, I give them away. When that worker gets the used car, you would think that I had given them a trunk filled with gold. They are ecstatic. But I can tell you, I have more joy in giving that car away than I ever received from buying it or even driving it. My heart benefits from it.

A person doesn't have to be wealthy, though, or even give large gifts. Even small tokens of generosity to a person in need can help their life and warm your heart. And the more we give, the more we want to give. It is one of the greatest joys of life. I often wonder about these folks who make millions and don't give money away to help improve the lives of others or to help with causes. What purpose does it serve simply to make your pile bigger and bigger? I have never been able to see it. And yet, ironically, the more I have given away, the more successful I have become. There is a lesson there, Josh. Lao Tzu put it this way: "The wise man does not lay up his own treasures. The more he gives to others, the more he has for his own."

Make it your quest to give as much as you can in your life. Spend your time thinking about how you can give rather than how you can get. In doing so, you create a wonderful life for yourself. A delightful little quote I ran across says it so well. It is by Francis Quarles. "The fountain of beauty is the heart, and every generous thought illustrates the walls of your chamber." Generous thoughts become generous actions. Let your heart and mind be filled with generosity, and your life will be as well.

One last thought. Do not be generous for what you may receive in return. Be generous because it is right. Francesco Guicciardini was right when he said, "The return we reap from generous actions is not always evident." You may never see the result of your generosity. That is okay. Be generous in order to do well for others and to keep your heart in the right place. If you see the result, great. If not, know that you are doing what is right and protecting your heart from greed.

7 Perseverance and Resignation

. . . .

The heart can grow weary, Josh. It can come to the point where it has encountered so many obstacles, for so long, that it gets tired. It can see so many times of sadness that it grows heavy. The heart has an ebb and flow to it. Certainly, when times and circumstances are good, it is easy for the heart to feel strong. The challenge is in hard times.

Jesus said, "In this world you will have trouble." Truer words were never spoken. All people experience trouble. It is part of the human experience. But in those moments of challenge, we again must look deep-down within us and make a choice about which of the two sides will control our lives. Will we face the struggle head-on, tell ourselves that with more effort we can succeed, and persevere? Or will we throw in the towel in resignation to the idea that the obstacles we encounter are too great and will keep us from the dreams we have? The choice we make will determine to a great degree what kind of success we have in life.

Building a business takes perseverance. Making a marriage work takes perseverance. Raising children takes perseverance. Securing your financial future takes perseverance. Anything worth doing will require a strong heart of perseverance.

There will be times in life when you will feel like you have gone as far as you can go and given all the effort you can give. At that point, I always heeded the words of Franklin Roosevelt: "When you come to the end of your rope, tie a knot and hang on." There were times when I said to myself, "Just one more day. You can go one more day." Or, "One more week. You can make it one more week." When I came to the point of having to persevere or to resign, I chose to persevere just one more time. And over and over again, that heart of perseverance carried me through.

Then, just when you have conquered one challenge, along comes another. There are many times you do not have time to take a breath. John Quincy Adams said, "Patience and perseverance have a magical effect before which difficulties disappear and obstacles vanish." This is true, but then they pop up again. Life is a series of overcoming obstacles. Oliver Wendell Holmes put it this way: "The moment you turn a corner, you see another straight stretch ahead and there comes some further challenge to your ambition."

Yes, no matter who you are, nor where you live, and no matter what your station in life may be, you will repeatedly be confronted with the decision to persevere or resign. To push on or to give up. You will fail from time to time, and that is part of persevering. Ralph Waldo Emerson said, "Our greatest glory is not in never failing, but in rising up every time we fail." That is perseverance.

Here is one of my favorite quotes of all time:

> *Nothing in this world can take the place of persistence.*
> *Talent will not; nothing is more common than*
> *unsuccessful people with talent. Genius will not;*
> *unrewarded genius is almost a proverb. Education will*
> *not; the world is full of educated derelicts. Persistence*
> *and determination alone are omnipotent. The slogan*
> *"Press On" has solved and always will solve the problems*
> *of the human race.*
> —Calvin Coolidge

America's first billionaire, John D. Rockefeller, placed perseverance at the top of the list of character traits this way: "I do not think there is any other quality so essential to success of any kind as the quality of perseverance."

Guard your heart, Josh, against the creeping enemy of resignation, the foe that will seek to make your life mediocre and average by convincing you that you can go no further. Make your heart strong with regular discipline in the good times so that in the not-so-good times you will have the strength you need to carry on one more time and come one step closer to your dreams and your full potential. This was what I did to become what I have become and to achieve what I have achieved in life. I am no better than anyone else. Anyone who will reach down deep within themselves can do the same.

Josh, I hope that these lessons will help you with your paper. Even more, however, I hope that you will listen to these words and apply them to your life. I have learned them by trial and error. I have learned them through the fire of testing. I have not always succeeded, but sometimes failed. When I failed, though, I learned from that failure and made the choice to move forward, learn from my mistakes, and reach my fullest potential. You can do the same.

- *Demonstrate humility*

- *Forgive others*

- *Be vulnerable*

- *Show courage*

- *Have hope*

- *Exercise generosity*

- *Persevere*

> *"Above all else, guard your heart, for it is the wellspring of life."*
>
> —Solomon

I can give you no better advice than that.

Love, Grandpa

EPILOGUE

* * * *

A few weeks later, Michael received an envelope with a letter inside from Josh. It read:

Dear Grandpa,

Thank you for flying me down to Florida to spend some time with you and work on my school project. I had a lot of fun fishing with you and spending time with you and Grandma. As I get older, I'm realizing how fortunate I am to have been born into our family.

I especially appreciated what you taught me about the heart. I know, as a kid, I probably don't think about it as much as I should, but it sounds like you say that adults don't think about it as much as they should, either. Hopefully, the lessons you talked to me and wrote to me about will be ones that I can use for the rest of my life. I will be sure to let you know what grade I get on my report!

Thanks again from your oldest grandson,

Josh

Three weeks later, Michael received another envelope, this time with just a card in it and a short note:

Grandpa, I got an A! Thanks! Josh

QUESTIONS FOR REFLECTION AND GROUP DISCUSSION GUIDE

.....

1. Would you say that you guard your heart "above all else"? If so, why? If not, why not?

_____

_____

2. How would you describe the "well" that your heart is?

_____

_____

3. How would you describe the current state of your heart?

_____

_____

4. In what ways would you say your heart has been a benefit or hindrance to your current state of success?

_____

_____

5. Would you say that you "guard your heart"? Why or why not? If so, how so?

_____

_____

6. What would you say is the focus of your heart?

_____

_____

7. In what ways do you currently foster the growth of your heart?

_____

_____

8. Think through each of the disciplines listed below, and reflect on how they could become more a part of your life and how they may improve your life:

   • *Solitude* _____

   • *Silence* _____

   • *Reading* _____

   • *Prayer/Fasting* _____

9. What are the obstacles you face in implementing these disciplines in your life?

_____

_____

10. What would you say are the major foes to the growth of your heart?

_____

_____

REFLECTIONS ON THE FACE-OFFS OF THE HEART

Humility and Pride

- In what ways do you experience the face-off between humility and pride in your heart?

_____

_____

- What are the tangible outcomes you experience because of the state of your heart in this area?

_____

_____

Forgiveness and Retribution

- In what ways do you experience the face-off between forgiveness and retribution in your heart?

_____

_____

- What are the tangible outcomes you experience because of the state of your heart in this area?

_____

_____

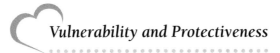

Vulnerability and Protectiveness

- In what ways do you experience the face-off between vulnerability and protectiveness in your heart?

_____

_____

- What are the tangible outcomes you experience because of the state of your heart in this area?

_____

_____

Courage and Fear

- In what ways do you experience the face-off between courage and fear in your heart?

_____

_____

- What are the tangible outcomes you experience because of the state of your heart in this area?

_____

_____

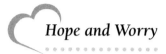

Hope and Worry

- In what ways do you experience the face-off between hope and worry in your heart?

_____

_____

- What are the tangible outcomes you experience because of the state of your heart in this area?

_____

_____

Generosity and Greed

- In what ways do you experience the face-off between generosity and greed in your heart?

_____

_____

- What are the tangible outcomes you experience because of the state of your heart in this area?

_____

_____

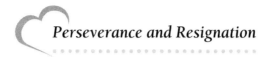
Perseverance and Resignation

- In what ways do you experience the face-off between perseverance and resignation in your heart?

_____

_____

- What are the tangible outcomes you experience because of the state of your heart in this area?

_____

_____

FROM HERE...

- After reading *Above All Else*, what changes will you make in your life? What commitments will you make?

_____

_____

- How do you see the lessons learned here affecting you in the following areas:

- *Family and Marriage* _____

- *Business* _____

- *Relationships* _____

- *Finances* _____

ABOUT THE AUTHOR

Chris Widener is an example of how anyone can overcome any odds to achieve a successful life and help others achieve the same. Chris has overcome many obstacles... living through his father's sudden death when he was four, being sent away to live with relatives at age nine, and becoming involved with drugs and alcohol by the age of twelve.

Chris overcame these obstacles, and has been speaking professionally since 1988. He has shared the stage with U.S. presidential candidates, nationally known television news anchors, best-selling authors, and professional athletes. Chris is a successful businessman, *New York Times* and *Wall Street Journal* best-selling author, speaker, and television host.

He has authored over 450 articles and nine books, including the *New York Times* and *Wall Street Journal* best-seller *The Angel Inside*. He has produced over eighty-five CDs and DVDs on leadership, motivation, and success.

Chris is the host of *Made for Success* and co-host of *True Performance* with Zig Ziglar. Chris is also a featured columnist for *SUCCESS* magazine.

The Chris Widener e-zine is one of the most widely distributed newsletters on personal and professional development. Personal-development legends such as Zig Ziglar, John C. Maxwell, Brian Tracy, Jim Rohn, and Denis Waitley have lauded Chris's work, and many consider him the leader of a new generation of personal-development experts.

Chris, his wife, Lisa, and their four children make their home in a suburb of Seattle, Washington.

CHRIS WIDENER RESOURCES

ACHIEVE A HIGHER LEVEL OF SUCCESS

Now that you've enjoyed *Above All Else*, explore Chris Widener's other exceptional works that provide life-changing principles of leadership, motivation, and success.

MADE FOR SUCCESS SERIES

Chris learned early on that if you're interested in achieving success faster and with fewer struggles, then one of the easiest ways is to learn how other successful people did it and simply… copy them!

This incredible DVD/CD set features in-depth interviews with twenty-three of today's most renowned experts in their fields, including America's foremost business philosopher, Jim Rohn, best-selling co-author of the *Chicken Soup for the Soul* series Mark Victor Hansen, San Antonio Spurs mental training coach David Cook, former NFL quarterback Tom Flick, former CFO of Microsoft John Connors, and many more. You get practical advice, ideas, tips, and training on:

Leadership • Goal-Setting • Time Management
Selling Techniques • Motivation, and much more!
23 DVDs/CDs

To order, visit *www.ChrisWidener.com* or call 877-243-8383.

TWELVE PILLARS: THE SKILLS YOU NEED TO SUCCEED

In this program, based on the best-selling book by Chris Widener and Jim Rohn, Chris walks you through the twelve pillars that will forever change your personal and business life for the better. A must-listen for all those in search of the good life!

7 CDs with comprehensive 132-page Study Guide Workbook

WINNING WITH INFLUENCE

Chris teaches the twelve characteristics of dynamic leaders, salespeople, and top performers. Learn what the successful already know—how to earn wealth, power, recognition, and influence that will change your life and allow you to live the life of your dreams.

8 CDs

INVISIBLE PROFIT SYSTEM

Learn from Chris how some of the world's most financially successful people have solved the "time for money" trap while also helping others become financially independent.

1 CD

To order, visit *www.ChrisWidener.com* or call 877-243-8383.

THE EXTRAORDINARY LEADERS SEMINAR

Make yourself into an extraordinary leader! Learn the character traits and skills of leaders, the ways to develop leaders, leadership myths and mistakes, and more!

13 CDs with Downloadable Workbook

THE ULTIMATE SUCCESS SERIES

Chris' definitive discussions on a variety of success and leadership principles. This important series includes the *Ultimate Time Management Seminar, Bringing Balance to a Chaotic Life, Live the Life You've Always Dreamed Of, The "Best" Test, Right Now Leadership—What You Can Do Today to Be a Better Leader, Finding Financial Freedom to Ensure a Fantastic Financial Finish,* and *Seven Minutes to Success.*

12 CDs

BOOKS BY CHRIS WIDENER

• • • •

THE ANGEL INSIDE

Journey to modern-day Florence, Italy, where a despondent 30-year-old American meets a mysterious old man who challenges him to take a deeper look at his life.

THE ART OF INFLUENCE

A powerful tale that shows that business success does not come from Ivy League degrees, but from an individual's own personal courage and commitment to succeed.

TWELVE PILLARS

This novel by Jim Rohn and Chris Widener will inspire you to take your life to the next level and beyond. It will challenge and encourage you to become the best that you can be!

To order, visit *www.ChrisWidener.com* or call 877-243-8383.

LIVE THE LIFE YOU'VE DREAMED OF!

Ten rock-solid principles that will absolutely, positively, turn your dreams into realities! Imagine what it would be like to have no goal unfulfilled and to know how to stay motivated—all the time! This amazing book is your ticket to the life you *want* to live.

THE IMAGE

Compelling and to the point, this book addresses questions that so many have struggled to answer in their lives. Chris Widener and his unique ability to weave vital success principles into a story will inspire you to go for it and to reach for your God-given potential!

CHRIS WIDENER'S TREASURY OF QUOTES

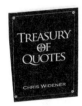

The quotes you'll find in this elegant little book are seeds taken from the collection of articles Chris has written over the years. Read them slowly. Ponder them. Ask yourself how they apply to you. Let the truths you find take root and grow into something magnificent in your life!

Each booklet has a special "To and From" section, making it a great gift for family, friends, and colleagues!

To order, visit *www.ChrisWidener.com* or call 877-243-8383.

The Leader of a New Generation of Personal-Development and Leadership Experts

· · · ·

For years, audiences have enjoyed Chris Widener's engaging, versatile speaking style and his ability to educate and train, while instilling humor, excitement and passion. For your next event or meeting, consider Chris Widener for the very best lectures or seminars on inspiration, leadership, success, and personal development. His topics include:

- *Winning with Influence – The Real Way to Influence Others*

- *Twelve Pillars of Success – Designing Your Best Life!*

- *You CAN Live the American Dream – The Dream Is Alive and Well and You CAN Live It!*

- *Extraordinary Leaders – Leadership Skills and Character Traits to Take You and Your Organization to the Next Level!*

- *Keys of Successful Teams – How to Turn Your Team into a Winning Team!*

- *Right Now Leadership: What You Can Do Today to Become a Better Leader*

- *Live the Life You've Always Dreamed Of!*

Chris is always happy to tailor his presentation for your organization to create maximum impact!

· ·

For more information or to book Chris, e-mail speaker@chriswidener.com or call 877-212-4747.